P9-DGE-489

Gardens of the Streets

Poetry and Pictures of
Urban Rescue Missions
and the People They Serve

William Lewis Clark

Mayhaven Publishing

Mayhaven Publishing
P O Box 557
Mahomet, IL 61853
USA

Except where designated,
the photographs in this book are by William Lewis Clark
or Jennifer L. Smith

Cover Illustration by Denny Rogers
First Edition—First Printing   1995   1 2 3 4 5 6 7 8 9 10
Superior Printing, Champaign, Illinois
Library of Congress Number: 95-77227
ISBN: 1-878044-40-0

Dedication

To Mom and Dad
for the seeds of love and faith
they sowed in my life.

Editor's Note

No effort was made to diminish the role of religious organizations in the care of the homeless and the needy. For the most part, they have carried the bulk of the burden for generations.

And little effort was needed to edit the poems of William Lewis Clark. His words reflect his artistry and his intimate and unique perspective on a world most others do not fully understand.

Foreword

There have been many great artists . . . who have attempted to paint what they believed to be the portrait of Jesus. The problem has been that the Black Christian, or Native American, or the Mexican, or the Oriental Christian has had a difficult time identifying with this pale-skinned . . . Messiah. In fact, some have rejected His gospel because of what they have seen . . . when I read the poems of William "Bill" Clark and look at the pictures and see the great work that so many . . . are doing every day because of their love . . . for God and His people, I see a genuine portrait of Jesus . . . Thanks, Bill, for a picture of Jesus with which we can all live.

Rev. Ervin Williams
Director/Pastor
Restoration Urban Ministries

Illustrations and Photographs

Contents

Introduction

Born in those sacred places in the city where human need and human compassion meet, American rescue missions have been a legacy of hope for millions of our citizens for over one hundred years. Countless numbers of men and women have turned in desperate times to a city mission as a last resort and been taken in, fed and given encouragement to go on. We must, as a nation, guard the trust and preserve the legacy and the future of the American Urban Rescue Mission lest there be a day when one man, one woman, or one child finds themselves in a place where there truly is no place to turn, where once stood the glowing welcome of a rescue mission.

This book came about from my desire to get to know, understand, and convey to others something of the lives and emotions of the diverse people who come through the doors of Restoration Urban Ministries, a mission in Champaign, Illinois.

Some of these people came and went and we never saw them again, and some came and stayed and became a part of our lives for a while — and a part of the daily life of the mission. I invite you to share with me the sentiments, the personalities, and the stories that I have attempted to capture on the pages of this book.

The lives represented here are not intended to inspire pity, for in many of them are chords of the irrepressible strains of hope infused by God into the human spirit. They are simply meant to present, as accurately as possible, a representative vision of the emotional world of persons who face, on a more immediate level than the general population, the struggle for survival.

So many of those that we help are those affected by three of society's most devastating problems: alcohol and drug addiction, physical and sexual abuse, and homelessness. Along with some insight into the missions and the people who serve them, these subjects comprise the divisions in this book. So often these three problems are not only intertwined in the lives and families we work with, but addiction and abuse become a plague whose roots go deep into preceding generations and reach out to scar the lives of future generations. Behind the statistics on these problems, documented by research and the media, are the actual lives we see each day at the mission.

William Lewis Clark—April, 23, 1995

The Gardens

William Lewis Clark—

Street People #1
Illustration by Denny Rogers

Street People #2
Illustration by Denny Rogers

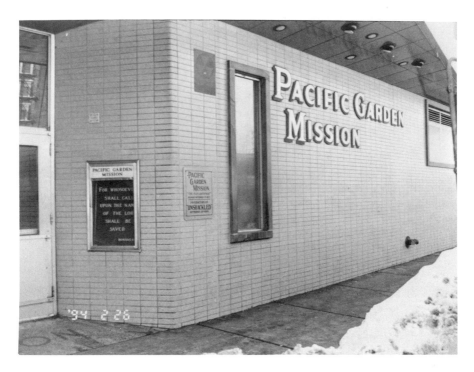

Pacific Garden Mission

Pacific Garden Mission, founded in 1877, is the nation's second oldest rescue mission. It ministers around the clock to Chicago's homeless and other destitute people. Pacific Garden Mission has a men's division, a women's division and a children's division; and originates the half-hour radio drama "Unshackled!" heard on more than 900 outlets around the world. Inside the mission, is a twenty-four hour Hotline phone taking crisis calls from countries all over the world where "Unshackled!" is heard.

18

The Mission

Each day they appeared —
often wordless in their need,
yet each one priceless in their worth.

A torch had been set outside this place,
and it had been declared God's.
And now each day beginning at nine o'clock
its doors throbbed with hunger.
Its doors throbbed with the needs and deprivations
of those who must try to balance
the weight of their worlds on the edge of a jagged hope.

And though there was never enough money,
they all somehow got fed.
And though there were never enough helpers
they all somehow felt the love
God held for them there.

And as for those who worked there,
they all knew the danger of caring for someone
who might disappear into the night
never to be seen again.
They knew what it was like
trying to comfort those
whose final days in unfinished lives
might be spent under the melting pity of icicles
in some hostile doorway.

19

William Lewis Clark—

They'd seen those unfit to carry their tragedies
still carrying them out on the streets,
and they'd seen pain
eyes could no longer imprison
trickling down in tears
creating somber scenes of life's hardships
on the canvass of worn faces.
Yet, too, they learned that there was life
in the smallest act of kindness.

And those who kept that torch lit outside that doorway
spent their days walking on water,
spent their days watching Jesus feed the five thousand
with five loaves and two pieces of fish;
spent their days watching
as Jesus healed the sick
of soul, mind, and body.

And each day God gave these workers
love enough to see through the tragedies
to the miracles;
the hope to wrap the warmth of caring around even one
trapped in the chill of neglect
until feeling came back to this one.
And so, too, the torch's reminder
that Jesus still cared—
Not Just two thousand years ago
but now,
here.

He was alive in this place
for these souls bubbling up to the surface of the light—
the fire of their testimony now on their tongue—
having found love
to heal the scars and bitterness of their lifetimes,
and grace
to lead them into the glory of their eternity.
And when the day was done
the torch still burned.

William Lewis Clark—

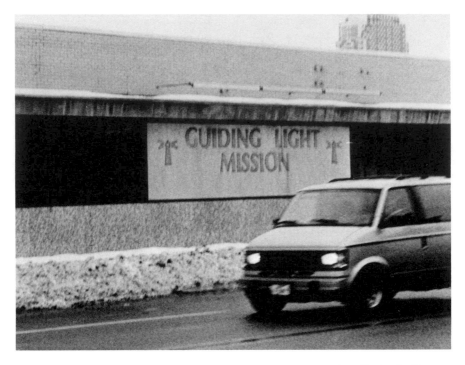

Jennifer L. Smith

Guiding Light Mission

A mission is not stagnant. It radiates its vitality into the community. It responds to the fray of urban life, saturating it with power and hope. A good mission points to the best possibilities of urban communities, and by serving these communities it spills out an internal strength, a commitment to the fragile human condition inside impoverished urban neighborhoods.

The Mission Hotline
The Eclipse of Life and Loss

A Tribute to Those Who Work on the Twenty-four Hour
'Unshackled' Hotline at Pacific Garden Mission

The stars are imbedded
deep within a dark winter's night,
on an eve so still
tomorrow can almost be heard approaching.
And though on duty,
sleep still finds me lying on a bed
made of layers
of my congregating dreams.

But like a splashing pebble in a placid pool of slumber
just past the turnstile of dreams,
the telephone of crisis I must handle
rings out its fretful toll
and I answer to a heartbeat that's
pounding out the rhythm of fear.

A voice talks nervously,
desperately of its need
to find distance from life itself:
It talks of a pain
that comes after the unbearable;
of thoughts that shadow the unthinkable.

23

William Lewis Clark—

A ravenous grief climbs out of her whispers
traveling across silent Midwestern prairies
and I let it run towards me
across sloping wheat fields swaying in the wind
gaining momentum in telephone lines
under the weight of a thousand blackbirds
pinned against the night sky.
And I wait until I feel the bitter poison of her soul
and accept it
into mine.

And I too
remember shaking
in the chill of sorrow
that seemed to have no limits.

And in my helplessness
God is there.
And my prayers are
blocking off the streets of her hopelessness,
waiting on a miracle.
And as my prayers reach the One
whose love has anticipated their arrival and prepared
an answer of tenderness from before time began,
I begin to hear more willing second thoughts
behind the double-locked doors of her soul.

—Gardens of the Streets

Slowly she seems to regain enough strength
to face hope,
slowly she is backing away from the tormented bargain
she's made with death.

And God's love alone is still blocking off the streets
of her hopelessness,
as I listen in wonder
from the other end of a telephone line.

———————————

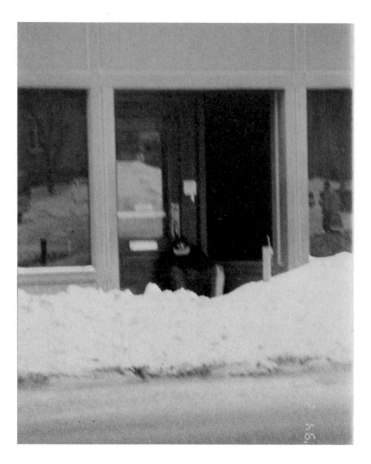

Jennifer L. Smith
The Doorway
"Thirty years ago if you saw a person lying helpless on the street you ran to help him. Now you step over him. You know he's not an accident victim. He lives there."

Charles Krauthammer

A World of
Repelling Forces

William Lewis Clark—

Jennifer L. Smith

No Loitering

"The thought of my pain, my homelessness is bitter poison.
I think of it constantly, and my spirit is depressed."

Lamentations 3: 19-20

The Simplicity of Love

Growing old on the streets
the soul shivers,
and memories soon become chains.

The fallen,
the homeless,
are conspicuous
by their constant presence
not their absence;
on display for all to see —
their frozen bodies;
the writing on the walls in winter.
In summer,
their lives the constant, obvious, plotting
to kill time in the sweltering heat;
minutes inching across a day,
the low, red sun seemingly stuck between floors.

In the shelter,
on a November night;
in row of shivering bodies,
a man named Walter,
fiftyish, with a greying beard
blue veins ignited by the stress of this coarse existence
are puffy under the skin of his forehead.

William Lewis Clark—

He lies motionless,
lifeless in his cot;
as if trying to conserve the will to live.

His life consists of exploring the distance
between hunger and survival,
between fear and terror;
while carrying so much loss inside him
he cannot convince himself
there is still room left
to feel love.

His memories fade back to the family he once had,
whose soft words filled the time
between his comings and his goings;
whose trust was the string around his finger
that reminded him to hope.

But then his wisdom
slowly evaporated in the whiskey,
and there were so many words that never got said;
and one day he woke up in the neglect he had inspired
that left him with nothing
to attach his life to
but the clock on the wall ticking.

And now there were only hours and days
left to pay his restitution
for letting life slip from his grasp:

moments of humiliation —
caught robbing a doorway of its warmth
and angrily expelled out into the night,
chasing a quarter and a cigarette down the street,
begging them to look him in the face
so they can see his unblinking desperation,
trying to find a safe place on the steam grates
not deserted by warmth
while the sirens seem to move closer
harvesting the night streets.

And then one night
slipping into the mission
along the back rows,
the rows for the skeptical
and those haunted by the vigor of their shame;
he hears the preacher
speaking in comforting tones,
his message almost finished.
He hears a story told of a Savior
that sheds light on the secrets of the life
he hides inside himself,
a life that has become a museum for the past
that he allows no one to enter.

He finds in this story the only truth, the only message
that can connect the memory of his past
with the life he now endures.

William Lewis Clark—

He can feel in himself a hesitant pull to move
from the back of the room
in the direction of the prayers
being spoken for him.
And the glow inside him brings back to memory
the strange simplicity
of love once more.

His eyes like sullied jewels
polished crystal clear
are reading the faces around him in the room,
and he sees kindness
and a gentle truth
in the eyes
of many there
that pour light into a future of grace
that beckons to him.

Secrets guarded
by knifing angles of self-protection
try to pin him
to his chair
and his hopelessness;

but as if rising to meet a miracle,
he stands at the preacher's call to come forward,
walking up front to accept God's freedom
and forgiveness; rising from his knees
into the glory of the eternal.

32

Packing Treasures For a Dream

Life is day-old cheap
on the East end
on the tracks
above the city.
Carrying a black plastic bag,
the greying
homeless woman
is excavating a rusting metal dumpster—
sorting through
Christmas ribbon
and beer cans
right under
everybody's nose,
pointed down.

She feels
like looking
into their soap-polished faces,
but she doesn't.
Brushing her hand
across her own face
baked by need
into a leathery camouflage
for survival,
she continues her chores.

William Lewis Clark—

A man glances at her
from a distance
avoiding eye-contact
like it could transmit disease.
He knows there must be something
he should do
to help
as he winds his watch
and then his parking meter,
as if to synchronize them.

He watches her
as she moves slowly down the street,
a parasite
on his contentment.

He wants to follow
but there's too much time on his meter
and not enough hours in the day
as he glances down again at his watch.
She moves into the distance
as twilight begins to fall,
searching for dinner
in a row of pay phones.

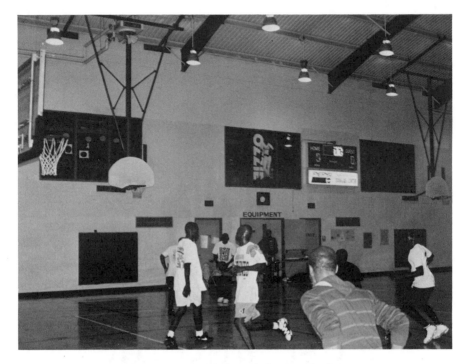

Restoration Urban Ministries # 1

Restoration Urban Ministries in Champaign, Illinois. A mission like Restoration Urban Ministries invests in the lives of people who enter its doors and in their futures. It affirms the value of people who oftentimes feel rejected by the larger society, and it challenges community residents to reach out for more fulfilling, more meaningful lives.

35

Choosing
Between the
Rush and the
Future

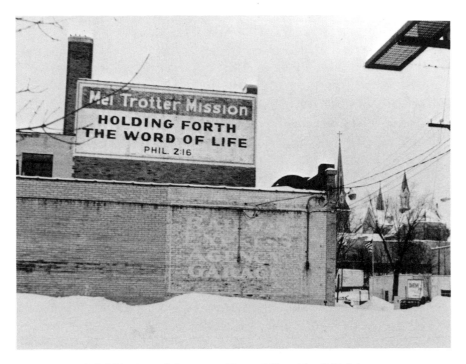

Mel Trotter Mission, Grand Rapids, Michigan

Mel Trotter founded sixty-nine missions. This was the first, founded in Grand Rapids, Michigan, in 1900. The mission has a detox unit, a crisis overnight unit, a residential program, and a family division.

William Lewis Clark—

Mel Trotter

Mel Trotter was an alcoholic. One day he came home drunk and found his little daughter sick. Instead of caring for her, he took off her shoes and sold them for one more drink. When he came home, he found her dead. Anguished and ashamed, he went out to end his life believing he was not worthy of living. He came upon a preacher talking about Jesus who loved those unworthy like himself. He was saved, and after gaining his own sobriety he went on to start sixty-nine missions in the United States helping tens of thousands of men and women to obtain sobriety and find Christ.

It is very difficult to argue with the awesome power of the gospel to transform the lives of alcoholics and drug addicts. In missions, this power is seen over and over each day. Bill Wilson, founder of Alcoholics Anonymous founded his twelve-step group on the principles of a Christian revival organization called the Oxford Group. He described his conversion experience that led to his sobriety this way, "I still gagged badly at the notion of a Power greater then myself, but finally, just for the moment, the last vestige of my proud obstinacy was crushed. All at once I found myself crying out, "If there is a God, let Him show Himself! I am ready to do anything, anything". . . . I lay on my bed, but now for a time I was in another world, a new world of consciousness. All about me and through me there was a wonderful feeling of Presence, and I thought to myself, "So this is the God of the preachers!"

Alcoholics Anonymous Comes of Age; A Brief History of A. A.

Restoration Urban Ministries # 2

"A mission offers the church, which has been mandated by God to serve the poor, the needy, and the broken-hearted, an opportunity and a vehicle to carry out this commission."

Rev. Ervin Williams.
Director of Restoration Urban Ministries

39

William Lewis Clark—

Leadership Qualities Inside a Maze

Fingers pacing the table-top,
his metabolism is set for rage,
the pain of his memories
is like a car horn
stuck and blaring after a flaming wreck.
Till death do us part
began the generic equivalent of their love.
And their wedding vows were like nonsense syllables
said before God in chilled whispers.
And thus they were welded together
frozen into a pose of financial convenience
and closed minded survival.

Their cold, drunken love is consummated
with clamps, forceps and tongs—
her body like a supple landing strip
for his cruelty.
There are no shallow scars in their world.
Only what the skin cannot defend against leaves a mark,
and only what the mind cannot defend against
leads to madness.
And finally in this madness
time gave birth to two children.
And savagely they still waged their war
as if all children were born deaf.
Her screams of fury wound the air around her
and scar the walls,

his hideous laugh
checking the children's reaction time
to horror.
And then one night she was gone.

With freedom embezzled
from their one common cause —
their stash of pharmaceuticals in the bedroom.
and with one eye puffy
staring back at her babies,
the other a falling star in a
distant galaxy of consciousness
refusing to see at all;
for her now
there was no turning back

Then it was just the old woman,
his mother,
who answered the ad of their need,
falling
into the jagged realm of his anger.
His disease now
always one word
ahead of his honesty;
coming home
drunk and drugged,
as she tried to wedge her love
between him and the children.

William Lewis Clark—

But she continued on,
thanking God for small miracles,
like when the dishes fell
and did not break,
as he rushed over
and examined them in the light.

She prayed that one day his
anger would coagulate into courage.
Yet she did not try to protect her heart,
the soft, bruised cheek of her forgiveness,
as she endured, trying to turn the clock back
to a time when they all looked up for hope.
Each day the resilient warmth of her smile
draped around his reclusive stare.

And each day his hate sprang up
in inebriated, explosive moments
branding doubt on the children's hearts.
At times he tried to pass down his illness
in angry kisses pressed against the lips
of the children's innocence,
but there the battle lines were drawn
and the old woman,
frail and bent by the harshness of her life,
banished him—out the door!
sometimes with little more than a soup ladle,
or a jar of kidney beans in her hands.

Every Sunday morning she dressed
up the children and took
them to the mission,
while he stayed at home
writing his prolonged obituary
in his father's drunken handwriting
—handwriting she knew so well.

And then one day she too was gone,
and it was if the whole world wore black.
But the seeds she had planted in the children's hearts
had taken hold,
and they whispered
at her grave side,
"Grandma we'll see you in that golden city,
with Jesus walking by your side."

William Lewis Clark—

"Is this not the fast that I have chosen:
To loose the bonds of wickedness,
To undo the heavy burdens,
To let the oppressed go free,
And that you break every yoke?
Is it not to share your bread
with the hungry,
And that you bring to your house the poor
who are cast out;

When you see the naked,
that you cover him,
And not hide yourself from your own flesh?
Then your Light
shall break forth like the morning,
Your healing shall spring forth speedily,
And your righteousness shall go before you;
The glory of the Lord shall be your rear
guard.
Then shall you call, and the Lord will
answer;
You shall cry, and He will say,
'Here I am.' "

Isaiah 58: 6-9

Jennifer L. Smith

The Lighthouse Deliverance Center

"I see violence and riots in the city, surrounding it day and night, filling it with crime and trouble. There is destruction everywhere; the streets are full of oppression and fraud."

Psalm 55:9-11

45

William Lewis Clark—

A Servant To The Flames

Drug-thrashed violence
sinks its teeth into the soft turf of the 'hood'
spitting out lives and scars—
the stitched measurements
for death's final fitting.

Upstairs in the shooting gallery
Franki's bangin' on the mud,
and hitting the rock,
working up a cold sweat
on a sticky Saturday night.

He gets each rush so easy
it feels like he ordered them
right out of the Sears catalog.

The seconds roll by gaining speed,
and one more time the urgent
gravity of the rock pulls him into its orbit.
Unsteady, he leans back against the bricks
choosing between the rush and the future.

Once again he mates with the crack,
and again feels the glowing conception
of a ten-minute lifetime
when sensation like a foaming waterfall
pounds the pleasure centers of his brain

a force worth dying for, worth killing for,
worth wearing iron for.

His heart begins pounding
a frantic, strobe electricity,
he fumbles for the pipe
then closes his eyes and hits it.
A crooked smile slides across his face,
then twists into a clenched tourniquet of fear;
it's midnight in his blood.
His senses contort
in some wild, chemical rodeo
that they can neither escape from
nor understand.

Suddenly, his body's a shiver-stick of reflexes
convulsing against a rocket's whiplash,
wild-eyed and over the edge
for the last time;
under the wheels of an overdose.

His brain lights one final candle
and then is convinced by the pain
to cease its inquiry
into the how's and why's of death.
At this distance, death is self-explanatory.

William Lewis Clark—

A World In Random Order

Put your ear to the door of apartment 207.
Inside a young boy, eleven,
comes out of hiding to probe the new day.

The disease of alcoholism
has burned a hole right through his family,
and now each member
is locked away
inside a strategy for survival,
constantly mapping out escape plans
from the closets of secrets they hide in.

The family has chosen
the boy to be the scapegoat;
to wear the family's shrink-to-fit shame.
They blister each other with their bitterness,
and then run off
to the private mirrors of addiction
to reaffirm their facades once more.

In the living room
his father sits
staring at the door.
He seldom speaks,
his grudging answers
seemingly
on ten-second delay.

—Gardens of the Streets

His skin-tight cravings
have led this family
into a crater of hopelessness,
and his wife into a fossilized
despair.

He studies her to avoid her.
When he must kiss her,
on birthdays, holidays,
her kiss is like picking
up a phone to a dial-tone
after it has rung
too many times unanswered.

The concealment of his arm-chair
is his only brace
against his guilt-splattered memory;
as he's trapped by the reunion
of his lies,
and cornered
by the tears and hate in his son's eyes.

Apples and
Arrows

From Dr. Conway

On a 1992 broadcast from the radio program *Focus on the Family*, Dr. Jim Conway, noted author and speaker, talked about the dysfunction in his life from childhood physical and mental abuse that continued to haunt him into adulthood. In the following excerpt, he tells of one incident of abuse and a little bit of how he began the healing process from the ravaging trauma of abuse.

[My counselor] said, "Close your eyes and let your heart just pick out a memory out of your past that is painful." And I closed my eyes and a flood of them ran by. And my mind kept sorting and sorting and finally picked out one.

When I was a child, my younger brother and I had done something wrong on a Sunday night. We had disobeyed my father . . . but my father found out and he got us out of bed that night and said, "You're going to get spanked on [next] Saturday morning." And He went out to the garage and got a stick . . . a board, a one by two, and he laid it on the corner of the kitchen counter where we went in and out, and he said, "As you walk by that, in and out every day, I want you to remember on Saturday you're going to get spanked."

William Lewis Clark—

The word was not spank; the word was beat. And it was this man, this two hundred and ten pound man, going to teach those little boys a lesson. And I remember that cruel experience. I was the first one to get beat. I was the compliant child. My father said, "Pull your pants down and lean over the bed." And then he started beating me.

I went into the closet just saying under my breath, "I hate you. I hate you. I hate you."

My brother was not compliant, would not accept the beating and he got beat all over his body—his head, his arms, just all over his body, being chased around the room like an animal.

Then [my] counselor said, "Now I want you to go back. I want you to go back into that room as an adult. Your dad is standing there. The two boys have gone into the closet for safety. Now go back into that room as an adult . . . and what would you say to the two boys?"

And I said, "I'd put my arms around them and say, 'Jesus is not like this man. Your father in heaven is not like this man. Don't ever believe that.' Don't throw God away with all the questions. You know, in the whole recovery movement, looking at secular and Christian alike, especially in the secular side of it, there is a sense of "after you get all healed and better, then you ought to tune in to this Divine Person."

I'm saying to you ". . . after you've decided that you need to be healed, then tune into God. See Him as your ally, helping you along through the process."

Adult Children of Legal or Emotional Divorce
by Jim Conway.
© 1990 Jim Conway.
Used by permission of
InterVarsity Press,
P. O. Box 1400,
Downers Grove, Illinois 60515

William Lewis Clark—

Suffer the Little Children

"But Jesus said, 'Let the children alone, and do not hinder them from coming to Me; for the kingdom of heaven belongs to such as these.' After laying hands on them, He departed from there."

Mathew 19:14-15

The House
Where We Hid Our Lives

It was as if home was a word we wore,
not the place where we lived.

My guilt rises up to light its candles
and sometimes
I can see clearly
back into the past
to our family,
that irreversible prefix to life.

I remember as
a small child,
ripped from
the embrace of innocence,
opening the screen door
on a summer afternoon
to my parent's screaming
and their fists.
Then after —
the sad, pale emotions;
seeing the cracks
for the first time
in the dingy wallpaper of our house,
and realizing that
life was surrounded
by edges I had never seen.

William Lewis Clark—

I can still feel
that first pricking memory
of being attacked
by something
l had no feeling for
but love.

And leaving a hollow stare
in the present,
I always go back
again and again
in search of meaning
from this leaking past—
always inside me
the fury of "why."

I see my fallen eyes
pruned of hope.
I hear their laughter
that always found me
in my hiding places.
And I look back on
the savage, drunken combat of their wills,
that was like some
bent, hideous opera
played out across a Sunday afternoon.

I think back on my brother
trying to pick me up from school on his bicycle,

because mother's face was too swollen
from my father's rage
for her to be allowed
out of the house.

My brother and I
locked each trauma
inside my father's rules of silence,
and were sent out with plagiarized expressions
to meet the world.
We learned that when we agreed
the pain never happened —
sometimes it would
leave by itself,
but sometimes then it
would feel like we
ourselves did not exist.

Some families you leave.
Some families
you must
dig out of.

I recall my mother's
fears and warnings
as I left,
trying to do her best to help,
yet her words just
passing down her shame

William Lewis Clark—

like passing down some physical feature
like freckles or dark eyes.

I learned from her,
from watching her anguish,
that a child's mind
keeps detailed records,
of the pain it endures.
Yet those records
often lie buried
deep within the soul.
And it's from those hidden graves
that the voices of childhood
echo their distress
in the lives of the victims of abuse.

And in the diary of my mind,
I remember the night
the police finally came;
and I can still picture
mother standing
in the front doorway,
half-insane,
trying to give them a full description
of the evil within
the soul of mankind
like she'd been waiting
for this moment
her whole life.

Her words still sting,
living inside me,
always asking to be seated beside me,
if for no other reason
but my understanding
of the agony within her.

Turning eighteen,
I left home;
a year before my brother,
not wanting to leave him behind,
but knowing I must—
not knowing how much
of me would also be
left behind.

We'd taken turns cleaning up after the madness,
We'd taken turns looking into the eyes of rage.
There were things we'd shared
of which we could never talk.

And I still remember that summer afternoon
at the screen door,
ripped from the embrace of innocence;
and even now, I enter each room and doorway
correcting for the fear;
correcting for the shame,
figuring out the shortcuts and the angles
to find the shadows.

William Lewis Clark—

Falling Backwards As I Write This
A Place of Forgiveness
Found In a Memory of My Father

The wind is lonely for a sympathetic ear.
Seven times I have flung open the window —
the fountain of the soft night breeze,
to let its currents flow against my skin;
suspecting that the night itself was listening
for footsteps of those not yet slumbering.

Recollections,
the insomnia of the past,
have gathered together tonight inside my mind
to seek release from their prisons deep within me.
Release that will only come from my forgiveness
of those who have wounded me.

Years living with the lies around me
were like acting lessons,
and you should see the best of my smiles.
But don't blame me for the tears I cannot hide.
Don't blame the wounds for bleeding.

And now tonight I go back there in my mind
where the lies began, where the echoes from the past
were spoken for the first time as words.
I go back to use words that I now possess

that can heal the pain inside me—
the phrases of forgiveness.

The echoes play in the shadows of my past
as I stumble back into yesterdays
following a prowling impulse
through unlisted numbers and
broken down basement flats,
through the drug years
and the years of hating,
of hating God and man.

And crawling through dark passageways.
Pain at times becomes my only reference point—
as I try to match it to
the hopeless despair
I've carried in my spirit
for so long.

Finally I find him,
the frost of permanence
still on his rejection,
his lower lip in that same snarled pose
I remember,
sitting out on the front porch
like when I used to come home from school
having to pass through that turnstile
of his bitterness and venom each day
and stiffen for his taunts.

William Lewis Clark—

But As I look at him
in my mind's eye,
his body is weaker now, more frail;
with signs of the cancer
that led to his death,
making obvious his mortality,
a mortality I had never noticed
when he was still living.

The glimpse of this weakness
brings out a sympathy in me that feels new,
and as I take the old man's hand in mine,
he looks up into my eyes.
Strangely to me, he doesn't try to pull back.
We start walking together
down that old dirt driveway,
his hand in mine,
and I speak to him gently
the words of understanding
and forgiveness that
God had taught me.
And slowly I feel the beginnings
of something inside me,
a hate deep down in my soul
slowly dying.

The bitterness and rage my father
left behind inside me,
as his father had left inside him,

has met a forgiveness
of mankind, that began
before the foundation of the world.
And as we walk together
my father and I,
down that old dirt road.
cup of forgiveness, quenching a thirst
that has lasted for
generations inside this one simple family.
We move on together
now within walking distance of peace.

William Lewis Clark—

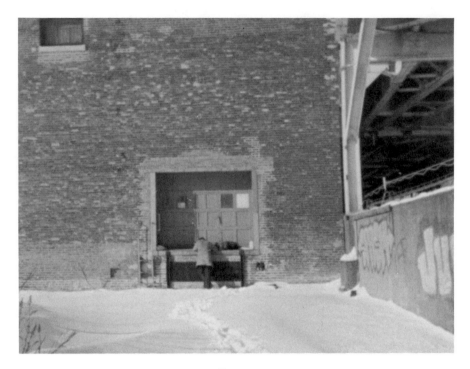

Doors

Missions today represent a place where men and women aren't left out in the cold, regardless of their beliefs or the nature of their problems. The role of missions is to serve and to express Christ's love even to those society shuns.

A World Staring Back

Over there, abandoned, a thirteen-year-old
stands grimly staring at his feet.
Just barely more than a child
though never a child;
raised on neglect and the blunt fist
of one father-figure after another.
Now, chased out of the apartment
one more time by the glaring face
of a man he barely knows,
he's trying not to feel disposable,
while sweating through a t-shirt
at a laundromat, killing time
'till he can sneak back home,
and "prosper" behind a locked bedroom door.

Letting the agility of his fear
guide him through a loophole
in his step-father's hangover,
he's through the front door
unnoticed,
testing the winds;
feeling the walls for forgiveness,
his eyes darting, searching for hope;
his ears straining for the tones of mercy
somewhere in the house.

William Lewis Clark—

Someday
there will be no more
father-figures.
Someday he'll rise up
and flourish inside his
true Father's love.

Melinda, 47, Incest Survivor

In Montana we have a plant, the farmers call it a weed, called a Creeping Jenny. On the surface its just a weed you can grab and pull out of the ground with your hands, and it spreads out across the ground; but the thing about it is, it has roots that go sometimes eight feet deep into the ground. There's no way to pull them out. They're like threads.

For a victim of incest the anger and the bitterness and the pain are like that. I can forgive my father for what he did, but the roots of that sickness go so deep that only God can enable you to get down all the way to your heart and get out all of that weed that is choking off who He created you to be. God says He searches our hearts and knows the hidden places. And He heals. The mission was an atmosphere where I could go and feel safe, and go through that whole process with people, with my family, and with the people there who turned into a family for us.

William Lewis Clark—

"To console those who mourn in Zion,
To give them beauty for ashes,
The oil of joy for mourning.
The garment of praise for
the spirit of heaviness;
That they be called
trees of righteousness,
The planting of the Lord,
that He may be glorified."

Isaiah 61: 3

Gwen

When the shadows breathed
next to my pillow
in the darkness,
it was him.
Out of the blackness
my father's brutal
unshaven face
would emerge,
his hands searching for me
beneath the covers.

And in that darkness
my fear would race ahead
of the moments I endured
trying to picture that final moment
when it would at last be over—
thinking of nothing more.

And as the shadows
breathed on my pillow
it was like one, two, three
flashbulbs clicking
exposing my innocence,
stealing from me my innocence;
leaving behind a permanent record
of humiliation and fear
in my likeness.

William Lewis Clark—

And I lay there,
helpless, frozen,
hanging onto the moon
outside my window
in fright.

And the facts would awaken the next morning
without a voice,
but with that same stench
of his stale sweat
sitting across from me
at the breakfast table.

And then some mornings
the facts would awaken
screaming out their story
only to be ignored,
upstaged by a plate
of bacon, toast, and eggs;
as mother sat there
never answering the pleas in my eyes—
the truth buried in a shallow grave
she kept well tended.

And like a young bird
who though sick and injured
must try to leave the nest nonetheless
the prodding of this sickness
in my father's mind led me to the

premature termination of my years
of service to hearth and home
at seventeen.

But there are so few
professions available
to those whose eyes
never leave the ground,
whose words get stuck in their throats
from choking on the memories.

I chose the one I had to
that let me hate that
little girl inside of me
so helpless and defiled
hanging
frozen to the moon.

I found I could rearrange
the names, the dates, the faces
and the moments in the madnes
of the drugs and Johns,
of a working girl
out on the street.

I found at times
I could live at a speed
one moment ahead
of all the weight

William Lewis Clark—

of anger and sorrow
inside of me.

Then one day,
the news reached me
that my father had died.
The feet of clay were at last revealed
on the god of my torture.
There are sins
and then there are abominations,
and though I tried to remember
the best of him
there was nothing I could lift from that grave
but the memory
of those nights of depravity
and that wicked smile
I saw through the darkness.

And so I, full of so many
words that needed to be
unburdened from my soul,
wandered into the mission
for its quiet and its temporary refuge
from the anger of the streets.

I carried with me the feeling
that somehow I should say
a prayer for his soul,
though not knowing

to which eternity
that I should ask it to be sent.

I longed to let this be the moment
I would take down that wall
of hardness and bitterness
I had built around me.
As I bent down on my knees,
I lifted up my eyes and looked towards heaven.

Simple words
inspired by God's Spirit
found the place of emptiness inside my soul
and sprung to life upon my tongue

"Jesus, people tell me
you died so I could live
forgiven of all I have done.
I've felt Your love here
surrounding me
for no reason I can understand.

Jesus, I have nothing to give you.
I live in a world where love is
bought and sold.
How did you ever find me there?

I have nothing to offer you
but my need to be healed,

William Lewis Clark—

my need to be saved.
Jesus you know how hard this is
for a person like me.
But Jesus I believe."

His grace came gently,
strangely different
than I imagined it,
and different from any kind of feeling
I had known before.
It was a grace that delighted in its giving,
whose joy was its mercy.
It was a grace whose beauty
was its righteousness
that contained no evil, no guile,
nothing but a blessing of a pure
and unspoiled love.

Clothed in His kindness
and His words of gentle healing,
my new Father began to tell me
of His love for me
and His care
even in my darkest moments.

"Gwen," He said,
"I cried for you
when you couldn't cry anymore.
I gave you courage to go on

when the darkness was too much to bear
for one so young.

"I grieve
with a sorrow it is impossible
for you to know
over the tragedies you suffered.
And I died to end this grip of sin
on mankind.

"I know how much you've suffered, Gwen.
I know the world of brutality
in which you have had to live.
I'll take you to a place someday
where those lies and those fears cannot enter.
You will learn to love, and trust, and forgive, Gwen,
and someday you'll realize
that I loved your father, too,
and in my mercy I had to wait for him
to have his chance to find Me."

I listened silently as He spoke
His words of peace.
He told me I need only ask
and He would begin the healing of my spirit.
He would teach me how to love again.
He would teach me how to finally blow away
the shadows.
And as I listened

William Lewis Clark—

with new hope entering my thoughts,
I began at last
to let go
of my frozen grip on the moon.

_____

A World Made of Corners

On the East-end,
in a room where the drapes never open,
a slumping man
in a pair of gray work pants,
dirt climbing the cuffs,
sits across from his young daughter
barely visible in the room's only lighting—
the ad-lib flickerings
of a television set.

She watches him—
looking back and forth
between his eyes
and the shot glass on the sink
in split-screen fear.

The tiny glass sits there
like a threat
as she waits,
knowing that out of that tiny crystal
pour the beatings and the depravity.

As the whiskey
winds the alarm clock of his rage,
anger flows up
from the bitterness inside him
and laps at her like flames from a burning building.

William Lewis Clark—

He hates her
because she has been contaminated
by fear,
contaminated by all
the times her love
has met the blade of his defenses.

Yet her unilateral attachment to him
is resilient, stubborn.
And the struggle continues,
pitting his cavernous
pain and brutality
against her innocence and forgiveness.

She searches the days and nights
for some sign of his love,
still guessing at the meaning of hope,
yet hearing God's whispers
of a coming peace,
knowing its not just the wind.

A World of Red Roses

Just twenty-seven steps from the mission
in a decaying brick hotel
worn almost into the abstract by time,
an elderly man is waking.

The heavy sleep
which stood guard last night
against his waiting, impatient grief,
is giving way to morning.

His slumber is parted
by cunning shards of sunlight
slipping into mischievous angles
as they pass through the blinds.

Sleep at last spills its brittle, aging cargo
out into a squinting consciousness,
out into the lonely sorrow of a widower
alone with his grief.

And he feels that familiar loss
once again,
as he begins wading into the undertow
of a bottle of cheap wine,
trying to focus on its blur
not its sting.

William Lewis Clark—

Once more
he finds himself
separated by a bottle
from all that could give him hope.

But the singing coming from the mission
makes him recall sitting next to his wife
in church with her in her favorite rose—colored dress
and with her voice rising up above the rest.

He thinks to himself
"How that woman loved her Jesus."
And he realizes at last
how she'd want him
to straighten his tie,
and straighten his collar,
and take that walk on Sundays
to worship in the Lord's house.
And in his mind he makes a solemn promise to her,
even now.

Sitting upon his bed,
he's looking out the window
out across the street,
living now just twenty-seven steps
from his future—
finally willing
to exchange her memory
for the lesson of her life.

Benediction

William Lewis Clark—

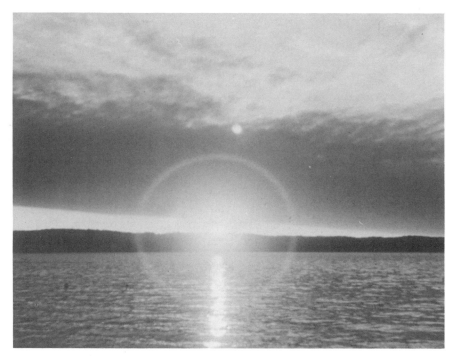

The Lamb

"And the city had no need of the sun or of the moon to shine in it, for the glory of God illuminated it, and the Lamb is its light."

Revelations 21:23

The Final Cherished Heart

As blessings from God's perfect heart,
there are angels that dwell among them—
His children,
the great harvest of His love.

And each one in this chosen gathering,
those born of faith and mercy,
will never walk
without a shining light along their paths,
and the comfort of God's Spirit
in their hearts.

A quest is set before them,
an urgency laid in their spirits—
to tell the story of their Savior
with tongues limber with faith and boldness,
and with words of conviction seasoned by walking daily
in the sacred footing of truth.

And in words inherited from the Spirit
they are taught the message
that in two thousand years has not faded—
a call to those still walking in the darkness
that points them to the path God so patiently tends
leading to His home.

William Lewis Clark—

And the stream of accent and imagery
proclaiming the same simple message of salvation
continues throughout the centuries,
a witness to that one magnetic truth, the gospel;
ages of countless voices
all giving expression to the same miracle of new life.

And though there is an eagerness
in all His children for His return
and the joy that awaits His reappearance,
yet an even greater wonder and awe
lies in knowing that He will wait,
His whole kingdom lingering in the balance;
until that final cherished heart
turns to find the warmth of His love.

". . . not wishing for any to perish but for all to come to repentance."

II Peter 3: 9

William Lewis Clark—

Mysteries Whispered To My Soul

When the dust pours again into our days,
who will outlive this world?

Our lives wane slowly,
yet are as fragile
as paper kites in a dream;
as delicate as the intersection of rainbows and sunsets.

But there are those,
the faithful, this subculture of the Light;
who carry a soul within them, predestined to live forever
in the presence of their glorious Savior.

Their names inextricably woven
into eternity in the Lamb's Book of Life.

God's Spirit has slipped faith inside their suspicions,
hope within their skepticism
and life eternal inside their former harmony
with a dying planet.

And too, there are those, who put an asterisk on miracles,
who can pierce the darkness only with a blunt doubting.

They are a consensus whose
lives are a voyage of the eyes only —
not sensing the unseen,

limitless dimension of faith
outstretched to meet them.

God's grace abounds above eye-level —
spilling out like the sun behind the clouds —
pleading,
yet it is unseen by those who
will never know the wonder
of thrilling in anticipation of eternity.

And as the dust again pours into our days,
this ritual of gravity continues.

And the drama of those lives unredeemed
spins by in revolving spheres of meaning
in lives performed a cappella,
without God's Spirit;

Sadly frozen in a denial
of the supernatural
until at last
finally crossing its borders.

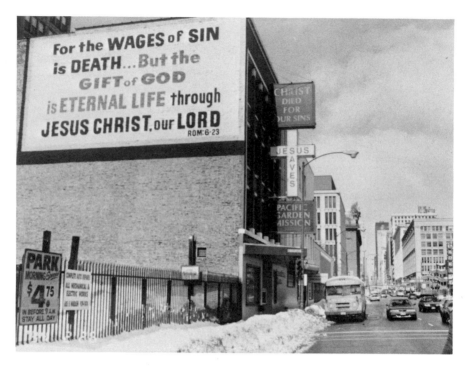

Pacific Garden Mission Sign

"The Spirit of the Lord is upon Me, because He has anointed Me to preach the gospel to the poor. He has sent Me to heal the brokenhearted, to preach deliverance to the captives and recovery of sight to the blind, to set at liberty those who are oppressed, to preach the acceptable year of our Lord."

Luke 4:18-19

The Silken Strand of Faith

Angels open doors for you.
Saints have laid bare their flights
from darkness into grace.
And the blade that sheers death
and darkness from the light
is sharpened to an edge by God,
ready to permanently sever you
from darkness
into His kingdom of life.

But you ask the standard questions,
and we pray
time stands still for you.
The prayers that the King of Kings
moves to our lips
filter out the chill of deception around you,
illuminate the shadow of mistrust within you,
steer your hand away from touching
the stairway to the wind.

For one fragile moment
we desire you to see
the true battle of the soul,
principalities and powers
striving with storm and fury;
the Holy Spirit gently bidding you
to let Him thread the silken strand of faith

William Lewis Clark—

through the needle of your doubt.
And even now the fallen angel of darkness
in their devouring madness
are trying to drag you into the labyrinth of unbelief.

And in His love He waits,
outwaiting our doubt,
outwaiting our apathy,
outwaiting all our attempts
to create a world
better than the glory
He has planned for us.

"Then the King will say to those on His right hand, 'Come you blessed of My Father, inherit the kingdom prepared for you from the foundation of the world:
for I was hungry and you gave Me food;
I was thirsty and you gave Me drink;
I was a stranger and you look Me in;

I was naked and you clothed Me;
I was in prison and you came to Me.'

"Then the righteous will answer Him, saying, 'Lord, when did we see You hungry and feed You, or thirsty and give You drink?

'When did we see You a stranger and take You in, or naked and clothe You?'

'Or when did we see You sick, or in prison, and come to you?'

"And the King will answer and say lo them, 'Assuredly, I say to you, inasmuch as you did it to one of the least of these My brethren, you did it to Me.'

Mathew 24:34-40

William Lewis Clark—

Rev. Ervin Williams,
Director of Restoration Urban Ministries

Rev. Williams represents the dynamic and compassionate
leadership necessary in today's complex urban settings.

The Author

William Lewis Clark is a graduate of the University of Illinois school of Journalism and presently serves as a Director of Drug and Alcohol Recovery at the Restoration Urban Ministries in Champaign, Illinois. This is his first book.